Healing Balm
Inspirational Reverie

Marjorie E. Favretto

WestBow
PRESS
A DIVISION OF THOMAS NELSON

WestBow Press books may be ordered through booksellers or by contacting:

WestBow Press
A Division of Thomas Nelson
1663 Liberty Drive
Bloomington, IN 47403
www.westbowpress.com
1-(866) 928-1240

ISBN: 978-1-4497-9279-4 (sc)
ISBN: 978-1-4497-9280-0 (e)

Library of Congress Control Number: 2013907310

Printed in the United States of America.

WestBow Press rev. date: 04/24/2013

To my husband, Reno,
for his constant love, encouragement and
unfailing faith in me, and to the Gift of Healing
we receive and give to one another.

HEAVEN'S PALETTE

Can you imagine God in His heaven,
Palette in hand,
Creating the colours
As only He can?

The Grass and the Trees
in the Spring will be Green.
Red and Amber for Fall,
a most glorious scene!

Golden for the Summer days,
Silver for the Stars at night.
Winter . . .
I'll leave Winter, white!

For the Oceans too,
A most beautiful hue;
They shall be Blue.
For Love, a very special glow;
I shall paint a Rainbow!

And then said God,
"I believe I'm done,
Enjoy my Masterpiece,
Everyone!"

UTOPIA

Oh, that we would all be blind
to the colour of our neighbour's skin.
Better still, with perfect vision,
we could recognize our kin.

And if his House of Worship
is a different one from ours,
Thank God at least, we both believe
in a Higher Power.

Only then and not until,
will the World know *Peace!*

HEART BEAT

In every heart,
There beats a song . . .

Celtic and Folk across the lands;
The Classics, the Opera
The World's Big Bands.

Beating of the Native drums;
Christmases' pum-rum-pum-pums;
Pop, Hip-Hop
and the latest craze;
Every generation
A new Phase.

Toe tappin' hand clappin'
guitar strummin' singalongs;
In every heart,
there beats a song.

I listen for yours.
Do you hear mine?

TEMPTATION

I never dip a toe in the pool
If I don't intend to swim.
I can be sure, if the water's warm
I'll want to jump right in.

And once I'm wet,
I'm bound to forget
all my good intentions!

THE COUNTRY LANE

Standing so tall
With our golden tresses
And brown speckled faces;
Queens in the fields
Encircled by fences.

Swaying in the summer sun;
Bringing smiles to everyone
who passes by
or chooses to run
barefoot,

Through our rows
Of Sunflowers.

MEDICINE 101

In Gramma's day, the cure for a cold,
A whopping dose of cod-liver oil.
You kept your milk on a block of ice
So that it wouldn't spoil.

In Gramma's day
wooden staves were used
to mend a broken leg.
On burns, they slathered bacon grease
wrapped up in old clean rags.

In Gramma's day, the country Doc.
dropped in, if passing by.
To check up on the family,
share tea and apple pie.

In Gramma's day, young mothers
gave birth in their own bed.
Up and about in a couple of days,
Doing chores and baking bread.
In Gramma's day they had precious little,
Their wants were very small.
But they had love,
They had it all!
So Gramma says.

FORGIVENESS

Trusting that our acts of kindness
and service that we've given
are the only deeds
that God records
In that Golden Book in Heaven,

Let us treat our failures
and those of our friends
With true forgiveness.

We tried;
God is satisfied.

STILLBORN

The sculpture,
Knocked from the pedestal
Just before the final touch,
Never to be admired.

The unfinished symphony,
never to
be heard.

The stillborn baby;
The beauty, the melody
Forever loved, forever played
In the mother`s heart.

GOD'S HEALING BALM

The warm rays of the Sun,
The beauty of Flowers,
The motion of the Ocean,
The magnificence of its Power.

The changing of the Moon,
The call of the Loon,
The spider web's design,
strength of steel, yet so fine.
The grandeur of tall Trees,
a summer Breeze.

Faithful pets, great and small;
The awesomeness of a Waterfall;
The Storm and then the calm . . .

Nature is God's Healing Balm!

On the Music score
Random notes are we,
Striving to become
The Melody!

PERSPECTIVE

To some,
A bothersome ugly weed;
To others,
A really good wine,

The much maligned
Dandelion!

MARITIMERS

If you love strolling on the beach,
Leaving your footprints in the sand,
Chewing on a piece of dulse,
digging for fresh clams,
You're probably a Maritimer.

If you delight in seaside rocks,
Sunning lazily on the docks;
Floating on a log or
Fishing in the fog,
If it really doesn't matter
long as you are near salt water,
You're probably a Maritimer.

I'm sure in Heaven, there'll be a Sea
With huge rolling waves for you and me.
Our Home for all Eternity,
because
We're Maritimers!

FRIENDS

Sometimes family fail the test
Of loyalty and steadfastness,
Its then, we depend
On old Friends.

Rare gems,
Hold on to them!

THE WEEKEND

Heading to the beach
On a sunny, summer Sunday
Three kids and the dog,
Raring to have a fun day.

A carload of beach chairs, towels and sodas,
Sand pails, swimsuits, and suntan lotion,
There's always something we forget
To take on our trip to the ocean!

Sunburned arms and legs and faces,
Two days later, still finding traces
Of sand, in places
It was never meant to be!

But we had a great time
And we'll do it again
Next weekend
For Shore!

THE SMALL TOWN BOYS

"Just running down to the Coffee Shop"
He said it every morning.
Meeting up with his old pals
In faded ball caps, trading stories.

Good old friends from grade school days;
Grew up in the same town,
Kept in touch throughout the years,
Through all their ups and downs.

Balding now, not quite so agile,
still playing "old boys" hockey;
a game or two of golf in summer,
consider themselves very lucky,

They're small-town boys.

SOLE TO SOLE

Part A

HI GAL, WHERE YA GOIN'?
Just to the mall.
MIND IF I JOG ALONG?
not at all . . .

I NEVER SEE YOU AT THE GYM.
No, I spend my time, shopping.
THAT'S NOT GOOD FOR THE SOLE!

Have you ever been to Paris?
NAH, BUT I WALKED THE MAYAN STEPS TWICE.
That must be nice.

WHAT SIZE ARE YOU? YOU'RE VERY TALL.
I used to be a seven; now more of a nine.
YEAH, TOUGH BEING WALKED ON ALL THE TIME.

SOLE TO SOLE

Part B

What do you do in your spare time?
OH, JUST KICK AROUND THE HOUSE.
Really! There's hundreds of us, I have my own shelf.
I CANT IMAGINE!
I'M AN ONLY PAIR, MYSELF.

That must be very lonely.
NOT REALLY, I GET TO GO OUT EVERY
DAY, MEET NEW SHOES . . .

Well I must be off . . . ta—ta
YEAH, SEE YA.

REVERIE

When quiet night embraces you
Just before you sleep,
In peaceful reverie
Pray to catch a glimpse
of the layered beauty
just beneath the surface
Of your soul,
Waiting for discovery

DAD

Seldom ill a day in his life,
Dad felt great at eighty five;
always glad to be alive.

It took a fractured hip
To lay him low.
He wanted to be up and on the go.

We did our best
to ease his stress.
Can we bring you this,
Can we get you that?

All he would say was,
"I miss my Cat!"

THE SEA OF LIFE

There'll be tears shed today,
And more tears tomorrow,
Tears of joy
Alas, tears of sorrow.

Tears of Gratitude
when a loved one recovers.
Tears of relief
when one discovers
his illness is curable.
Tears of frustration
to the new paralytic;
Tears of suffering and pain.

Tears of happiness,
Tears of helplessness
to be listed as critical.

Tears of joy
when a mother learns
her little boy
will walk again.

These are the Tears
That flow
Into the Sea of Life.

SUMMER VISITOR

Early morning dew
Glistens on bright hue
Welcoming you,
Little Humming Bird

I watch very still
While you sip your fill.
With lightening speed
You dart away,
and return a hundred times today.

And I am honored
You visit my garden
To find me,
Every summer.

HOPE

Huddled under worn out blankets
Lying on a sidewalk grate
How did I meet this terrible fate?
In fingerless mittens
Clinging to a beggar's cup;
Praying strangers fill it up
So I may eat today.

How did I go from three piece suits
And alligator shoes
To worn out boots with holes in the soles
And a brown paper bag
'Round a bottle of booze?

A loving wife; success in life
Before I was a "User".
Now a degenerate,
A "Loser,"
Alone.

Gazing at me with trusting eyes
My faithful dog, my only friend
Stirs within me, Hope
That once again, I can become
A Man!

HER SONS

As she looks upon her grown-up sons,
She sees the faces of her two little boys.
No more tricycles and skinned knees;
Today they play, with bigger toys.

One loves flying his own plane,
The other, racing cars.
She's been so blessed that neither son's
been called to fight the wars.

She thinks of all the mothers
Called to make that sacrifice.
And prays their sons will all return
From the battlefields, alive.

THE SPORTS FANATIC

He claims he's not a "Sports Fan"
Not "This" man!

Never misses football, baseball
Soccer, golf or basketball;
Classic games and recaps,
The weekly specials and the stats.

He'll swear to almost everyone,
My family mean the world to me!
(As long as there's no sports on TV)

But he's not a "Real Sports Fan"
Not "This" man

Just ask his wife!

ANGELS

Angels watching over us
Walking beside us,
there to guide us.

Granting protection,
In the trials we face;
Loving direction for
The choices we make.

Wonderful healers
In our pain and our strife,
Embrace them, welcome them
Into your life.

They know only Love,
They dwell in the Light.
Faithful guardians
By day and by night.

Angels, watching over us!

HOW ARE YOU?

When we ask a friend, *"How are you"*
Do we really want an answer?

Do we really want to hear
About their worries and their fears?
How they soaked their pillow thru' the night
with their never-ending tears.

Do we want to let them tell us
They've been diagnosed with cancer;
That they've just been laid off work
and they don't have any answers . . .

Do we really take the time to see
behind their frozen smiles?
Are we ready to walk with them
the next hundred fear-filled miles?

Or do we say *"How are You"*
and not really want the answer?

OLD GAL'S LAMENT

Shut down the theatres any day,
Who cares if they tear down the mall?
But Heaven forbid,
They close our Bingo Hall!

TALL SHIPS

Ghosts lingering in their bowels,
Tall Ships sail into harbour.
Cheering crowds along the pier,
waiting to board,
hoping to hear
the whispers of the Spirits;
of days of yore,
of all the wars,
fought beneath their sails.

In the misty morning fog,
Another journey in the log,
They head out for the seas,
returning home.

Their secrets,
theirs alone!

A PLACE IN MY HEART

From the first flutter in my womb,
I claimed you,
I named you
a *"Place in my Heart"*.

On your first day of school
we parted in tears;
Already five years, in this
"Place in my Heart."

Teen years, college
marriage and motherhood;
my "child" no longer . . .
Love only grew stronger
in this *"Place in my Heart."*
Tho' fate has placed us miles apart;
You're always as near,
always as dear
in this" *Place in my Heart."*

EIGHTY

"80" sits in a crowded room
apart from all the chatter.
He knows the family think him odd,
to him, it doesn't matter.
"80" lives in a quiet place
of Peace, within his soul.

A tear or two slide down his face
for the yesterdays he can't replace.
His memories are his alone
of his beloved wife.
and a happy home . . .

Quietly resigned to growing old
To let the last of his days unfold.
"80" knows a quiet joy;
a Peace within his soul.

SUMMER

Oh, the Joy of July!
Biting into softly ripened,
crimson peach skin,
Rivers of juices
Running down my chin!

Perhaps akin,
The chirping of the chickadees,
Intoxicating aroma
of the lilac trees.
A midnight swim,
the moon above;
What's not to love!

A new gift every day,
That's the way
Of Summer!

WISHING

When she was just a little girl
She couldn't wait to be sixteen
and wear bright red lipstick.

When she was a teenager,
she dreamed of finding
the "Love of her Life"
and having her own babies.

When she was a young mother
she dreamed of the day she'd have
grandchildren to cherish.

Now she's a grandmother;
She dreams of being that young mother
who would like to be the teenager
who when she was a little girl
just wanted to wear
bright red lipstick.

HAVE WE MET?

Why do we hide inside our shells,
afraid to show our real selves?
Do you think you know Me,
Know who I am,
Or are you a sham, as I am?

If we would open up our heart,
Unleash the fears that keep us apart,
You would no longer be a sham
and I could be who I am.

The phony you, would cease to be
and I could be the real Me.
We would then be fully alive;
Trusting, loving, Godly wise!

I LOVE YOU . . .

It's all the little things you do,
Like picking your clothes up off the floor;
Remembering not to slam the door
While the baby's sleeping.

It's all the times you try so hard,
To make me laugh; to make me proud.
The private glance across a room,
the phone call, or a tweet at noon
just to say "I Love You"

It's all the little things you do
that make me love you.

THE PAINTED WORD

Viewers at the gallery
Gaze in awe at the Veteran's canvas,
searching for the meaning.

What story is he telling?
What, the inspiration
behind his painted image?

Somber colours,
random splashes of red.
His memories of the war?
of the dead?

Does his painting speak his sorrow?
Is the bright flash of yellow
his hope for tomorrow?

Our homage to his artistry
we take our leave;
We feel we've seen
into
The Hero's Soul.

MOUNTAIN MAJESTY

Peaceful giants in your silence
Loudly praising God's magnificence.
Home to the elk, the deer and the bears,
Waterfalls and Trees
For billions of years.

Refuge to the hikers on your trails,
Delighting in your quiet place
Opting to escape the urban pace.

Ageless, timeless faithful giants,
Loudly praising God's magnificence,
We bow to your Majesty!

MY FRIEND

Only seven years old when we met each other;
Played with our dolls, grew up together.
Traded secrets in our teens,
spent hours together, in between
boyfriends.

Two busy young mothers,
always there for one another.
Years passed by, our children grew;
Friendship waned but rekindled anew
in our senior years.

I visit her now in a nursing home;
Her eyesight's faded,
Her memory's gone.
Like a little child she giggles, she cries
As she struggles to recall days gone by.
She remembers my name;
She's not sure why I came
To see her.

I long for the times that used to be
When we sat and chatted over tea.
Somewhere, in there,
The girl I once knew.

My Friend,
I miss you!

Home may be a seedy slum,
Home may be a mansion,
To God, it matters naught;

He makes His home
in the humble heart.

VISITING HOURS

I'd like to see a poster
In every patient room;

*"WHEN YOU COME TO PAY A VISIT
DON'T BE THE VOICE OF DOOM"*

Don't tell them of your aches and pains;
Of friends who passed away.
Just bring your smiles and try to help them
Have a better day!

LOVE YOU, MOM

"She'll be gone by morning,
You should say your good-byes".
Round her bedside, we hugged,
we cried.

We love you Mom; we understand,
We stroked her brow,
We held her hand.

With Peace her companion,
The long night passed.
In the very early morning
Mom breathed her last.

The Angels in Heaven
Today are blessed.
They welcomed our Mom
She's now at rest.

But, how we'll miss her!

PARTY TIME

Just teens, so young,
The Party such fun.
Kegs of beer, drugs galore;
Drink up man; have one more!

Staggering out, they jump in his car.
"I don't really have to drive too far" . . .

Oh God, what was that?
Did my car just crash?
I hear a siren somewhere in my head;
Where is my buddy?
Oh God, am I dead?

Please Mom, don't cry;
Don't ask me "Why"
I know you told me
Don't drink if you drive.

Oh God, I'm so sorry,
Please don't let me die!

ETERNAL MELODY

A thousand Angel voices
stopped singing on the earth
the day that Whitney died.
And we cried.

And the choir in Heaven
was never more beautiful
than the day
that she arrived!

SILENCE

Silence is not just the absence of sound;
In depression and loneliness
With noise all around,
There's a Silence.

Not understanding the cards
they've been dealt,
They long to be part of the joy
they once felt,
Before the Silence.

Let us hope and pray
As we hold their hand,
That the sun will shine
once again

Into the darkness of
their Silence

A DAY IN THE LIFE OF MY DOG

To the park;
Bark, bark, bark;
Off his leash,
"I'm free, I'm free"!

Chase a squirrel up a tree,
stop at every bush to pee,
play" chase a stick,
bring it back quick
Lets do it again
And again and again!"

On the sofa, half asleep
until he hears a bag of treats;
Tail a-waggin, he's on his feet!

Telling the time by his built-in clock
At ten he'll grab his favorite sock,
Then off to claim my bed!

TOGETHERNESS

In the winter of her life
she remembers the summers,
she remembers the springs
and all the wonderful things
they shared together.

She remembers their travels
and places they've been.
She remembers the good times
and the many times when
they laughed together.

She remembers how often
He said, "I love you"
She remembers she said
"I love you too" when
they loved together.

In the winter of her life
all her "Remembers"
are all their "Togethers"

Now that he's passed on . . .

A "CUPPA"

Three o'clock in the afternoon.
No matter what you're doing
Stop and put your feet up,
It's time to do some brewing.

Forget about the decaf,
Make mine real tea.
It's time to have
my pick-me-up
Won't you join me, please?

The chores can wait till later,
Put that work on hold.
Time to drink a cuppa
Before the pot gets cold!

THE SMILE

The "Smile" . . .
As precious as gold.

Let's afford ourselves,
the luxury to spend
And then my friend,
Together,
Watch the world
grow richer.

THE WIDOWER

Every day, at crack of dawn
He gets out of bed,
Puts his best suit on.
He visits his wife of sixty years,
Covers her gravestone with his tears,
Spends an hour, leaves her flowers.
So lonely now,
He just can't wait
To meet her again
At Heaven's gate.

RUN RUN RUN

Why are we running at such a pace
So anxious to get to that "other" place?
Are our goals really worth the race?

Life will unfold as it's meant to be.
Do we just waste our energy
Trying to outrun
the Speed of Life?

FISH TALE

Did you ever wonder how it looks
to the fishes' eye
to peer up through the frozen lake
And see the skaters whizzing by?

When spring time comes, without a doubt
They'll be peering up at the bottom of a boat
and see the fishermen, rod in hand;

Their future lying
in a frying pan!
POOR FISH!

GIFT OF TEARS

Spend time with folk in their senior years;
Just see how often they shed their tears.
Do you wonder why?

They cry for joy at the birth of a child,
They cry when you bid them "goodbye",
They cry with delight at
aurora borealis at night.

They cry at weddings
And at the funeral home.
They cry in public
Or when they're alone.
They even cry for strangers who die,
Do you wonder why?

They weep unabashed, their river of tears,
While they bask in the freedom of their aging years;
Freedom to wear their heart on their sleeve
And I believe,
They've earned it!

DID I?

At the end of the day
Did I remember to be kind?
Did I stimulate my mind?
Did I tend to my body?
Did I hurt anybody?

Did I learn any lessons?
Did I give thanks for my blessings?
Did I respond to God's grace?
Did I make this world a better place?

Did I serve the Lord?
Did I keep His word?
Did I pray?
Did I play?

or
Did I miss the chance
to celebrate the dance?

FOOLS EPITAPH

Life's Ambition: FINDING WEALTH

Last Admission: LOST MY HEALTH

ALAS!